AF426109

Being

ANGEL ANTHONY CORDERO

MILTON & HUGO L.L.C.
1001 3rd Avenue West, Suite 430
Bradenton, FL 34205, USA

Website: *www. miltonandhugo.com*
Hotline: *1- 888-778-0033*
Email: *info@miltonandhugo.com*

Ordering Information:
Quantity sales. Special discounts are granted to corporations, associations, and other organizations. For more information on these discounts, please reach out to the publisher using the contact information provided above.

ISBN-13:   979-8-89285-728-4   [Paperback Edition]
              979-8-89285-729-1   [Hardback Edition]
              979-8-89285-727-7   [Digital Edition]

Rev. date: 02/19/2026

Acknowledgements

"A special thanks to my colleagues Olivia Cahn, Isaac Griffin, Emily Huff, Riley Lavelle, Audrey Mahoney, J. Ridge Matthews, Tori Moskowitz, Alyssa Pallini, Prionti Talukdar, Justin Tison, and our outstanding city manager Luisa Estrada. You all inspired 7 Minutes and from that work *Being* was born. I treasured our time together in the Spanish days of Valladolid, and I sincerely hope our paths cross in the future. Sorry for making you all wait so long, but here is that second book you saw me working on after our long days of medical shadowing."

"To all those who were, are, and will still be I give these words that they would reflect on what was, is, and is to come."

"Beauty surrounds those who are brave enough to pursue her."

Preface

"To my readers, welcome back and thank you for all your support. Within these pages you will find plenty of new stories to resonate with and also change. I encourage you to change them by reading them not only as they are, but rather as what you would want them to be. As for the stories I have chosen to revisit, I pray you would enjoy changing them and updating the narratives you created the first time around. *Being* in many ways is a companion to *The Life We Lead*, but it is also meant to stand on its own. I welcome you all once again to come on a journey with me. Come along and experience *Being*."

Contents

NOSTALGIC

7 Minutes

What if we live our entire lives for 7 minutes?
Perhaps, in the grand scheme of things, all we do is pass through life gathering memories for the end.
Maybe, just maybe, it is the pursuit of a beautiful 7 minutes that causes us to push past our limits.

What if the essence of our being is not who we are, but the friends we make along the way through our travels and visits?
Perchance it is those strangers who become friends who become family that our memory sends for at the end.
What if we live our entire lives for 7 minutes?

What if it's the family we make along the way, not the one that was given that matters as we sit there in solitude with the next life having already punched our tickets?
Perhaps that is the beauty of life; in a span of time that at first seems insignificant, we come to author stories that weave themselves into our souls.
Maybe, just maybe, it is the pursuit of a beautiful 7 minutes that causes us to push past our limits.

What if it is the first short and insignificant moments, we remember at our final sunset?
Perchance it is in those moments shared among strangers who became friends who became family that the most beautiful chapters of who we are come to an end.
What if we live our entire lives for 7 minutes?

What if who we are is beautiful not because of us but because of everyone we have met?

Perhaps that is the true gift we all share.

The ability to laugh and love and care for each other before it all ends.

Maybe, just maybe, it is the pursuit of a beautiful seven minutes that causes us to push past our limits.

Yes, maybe our lives are or are not lived for anything more than 7 minutes.

Yet, when it is all said and done, I hope that in those 7 minutes my last bit of consciousness will bring me memories of you.

What if we live our entire lives for 7 minutes?

Maybe, just maybe it is the pursuit of a beautiful seven minutes that causes us to push past our limits.

Nostalgia

You let our souls remember the good times we had.
You let us recall the times we were glad.
A simple breath of memory carried by the wind.
A gentle word more precious than gold and diamonds.

Some say you come at the worst possible moments.
I say, "You come when we must reminisce."
Yes, you help us feel the emotions of time long past.
I know nothing so beautiful as making an emotion last.

You are the moment where everything stops.
You are the emotion we feel as our heart drops.
A rush of feeling straight through our hearts.
A shattering pull at the core of who we are.

Nostalgia, you give the best gift in the world.
Nostalgia, you let us relive the stories we told.

I Know Myself Now: Day 1

It's good to see you again.
It's time for me to tell you another story.
I've waited a long time.
Well, now you will wait no longer, let us begin.
Yes, please, let us begin.

Now, for the story of an artist and their muse.
Has this story not been told many times before?
No, this is the first.
Maybe for you, but others have told it before.
Well, it's a common trope.
Exactly, then why make me travel all this way?
Stick around, and you'll see.
If you say so, although, it simply makes no sense.
It will, eventually.

Well, my journey was long and I'm quite tired.
I see, well then what do you suggest?
The same as you suggested the first time you told me a story.
Okay then, I'll let you off to rest; I'll see you soon, precisely
tomorrow at noon.

I Know Myself Now: Day 2

Well, by now you know me.
Well, of course I know you, then again, who doesn't?
I guess that's fair enough.
Yes, shortly after our first meeting, you published.
Yet, you called me here after all this time, for what?
To tell you the story.
Yes, we proved that yesterday, did we not?
So then, why do you ask?
Because, since yesterday and today, nothing.
Fine, fine then, here it goes.

The words I published are the story I'll tell.
Tell, or already told?
Tell, it's time for someone to know about my muse.
Yes, your lady in red.
Yes, my lady in red, my opening wasn't exactly subtle.
No, no it was not, but that's a story for tomorrow.
Why tomorrow, must you leave so soon?
Not really no, but I want to review your first works and see if I
can find your muse.

I Know Myself Now: Day 3

Funny, noon once again.
Well, you left so suddenly, so I just guessed.
Tell me, who is my muse?
Well, I couldn't find her name, but she's an artist.

Well done! Let's start our story from the beginning.
I did not plan on love.
I didn't even plan on a muse.
I mean, how could I?
In my mind, I had stopped writing long, long, before.
Before her, in a time long gone.
I had run out of stories to tell and to write.
Then, I was proven wrong.
I was face to face with a new story to tell.
So, I lifted my pen.
I started to write again.

She seems to have inspired a great deal.
Yes, you could say that much.
What made her so special, what did she awaken?
Art, calls to other art.
Mystery always calls other mysteries.
Poetry, calls poets.
Most of all, passion ignites other passions.
What did she awaken?
She awoke the final embers of fire in me.
My final poetry.
She brought out the remaining stories I will tell.
Stories of hope and love.
Stories to inspire people, to give them dreams.
Stories that light up hearts.
Stories that will live long past me and long past my time.
We the readers owe her a great debt then.
Yes, you all do, she helped me find myself.
Really, who are you then?
If you can come, I'll tell you tomorrow at ten A.M.

I Know Myself Now: Day 4

Here I am once again.
Here you are, time for me to answer your question.
Yes, who are you, my friend?
I'm a poet blessed to know love intimately.

You're a poet blessed to know love intimately?
Yes, that is who I am.
Okay, but what does that even mean, I wonder?
Okay, let me explain.
As you know, I believe love has many faces.
Yes, that much I do know.
Well, to know love intimately is to know them.
Them being the faces?
Yes, the faces of love and everything they show.
All their grins and their frowns.
Their fleeting glances and their ice-cold stares.
The wrinkles they all have.
Yes, my friend, knowing love is knowing all of this.
Every little bit and piece.
I know them, so yes, I am the poet I say.

Well, my friend, your story was well, well worth my time.
I'm extremely glad I came.
Once again, you didn't disappoint, and I'm glad.
Wow, simply amazing!
Now all that's left is to decide when next to meet.

Well, I guess you're the listener, so you tell me.
I have 1 day left in town.
What about tomorrow at noon for old time's sake?
I'll be here; there is still one last part to this story that I have
left out.

I Know Myself Now: Finale

So, what have you held back?
Nothing has been held back; it is only untold.
They sound the same to me.
Fair enough, you have a point, they are quite the same.

Okay, enough of this game; I came for a tale.
That you did. Here it goes:
The best stories will always, always write themselves.
Poets are just vessels.
We sit waiting for the next story to be told.
The next dream. The next muse.
Then, we take that story and tell it as our own.
Yet, it was never ours.
The best stories have no owner, they stand alone.
They seem to change, adapt.
The poets who pen them are only their mirrors.
They want, but do not need us.
Because of this, poets understand what love is.
It's crazy, but it's true.
To be a poet is to love and to be loved.
To win and to lose.
It's feeling the highest highs and the lowest lows.

An interesting life it is that you lead, my friend.
It's entirely odd.
Yet, I can understand why it appeals to you.
Though, I wouldn't want it.
Anyone can be a poet, but at what cost?
Everything, everything!
Still, I would not trade being a poet for anything in the world.
If not for my being a poet, you and I would have never met.
True, and I wouldn't have heard such wonderful tales.
Yes, such wonderful tales, and many to come yet.

A POET

Misinterpreted

The beauty of poetry, as in life, lies in between the lines.
In the moments too often looked over.
In the words too often said haphazardly.
In the spontaneity of it all.
Yet, due to this, so often the very message is lost.

To understand poetry is to understand you know both everything
and nothing.
It is to understand that everything is right in front of you and
hidden.
It is knowing something to be both obvious and inconspicuous.
It is believing everything and doubting anything.
For poetry is where reality and fantasy cease to be separate
entities.

The beauty of life, as in poetry, lies in the unpredictability of the
story.
In the twists and turns, you never expected.
In the ups and downs you could never plan.
In the hills and valleys, you did not anticipate.
So, then I say that poetry in many ways is life.

To understand life is to understand poetry.
It is to understand that you will not always know what you think
you know.
It is to believe beyond what you can see.
It is to hope beyond the horizon even when the horizon seems to
run out.
Or tell me, is life not just as gray and also as colorful as the
mixed emotions and soulful feelings of the best phrase?

Yes, both life and poetry can often be misinterpreted.
Every moment is a new one we have never seen, just as every
phrase is a new turn we never anticipated.
Every breath is another chance just as every word is another step.
Every day is another sunrise just as every page is another
beginning.
Yes, both life and poetry are often misinterpreted, but to those
who find their true meaning a gift is given that can never be
stolen away.

Unappreciated

Criticism is the easiest of all art forms that anyone can create.
It takes little skill, less creativity, and practically zero talent.
All criticism requires is the ability to be afraid of something new.
Critics are unkind to the new for the same reason skeptics fear change.
Critics cannot accept that something may be more valuable than the entirety of their words designating it so.
Criticism in many ways is the ugly child of everything we have dared to give the sacred title of art.

Criticism is why the world needs her artists.
She needs those of us bold enough to dream.
She needs those of us crazy enough to believe.
She needs those of us wild enough to dare.
She needs those of us compassionate enough to care.
She needs those of us willing to jot down our stories and share.

See, a world without artists is one where the only voice is that of critics.
It is the world where dreams go to burn out.
It is a world where beauty is nowhere to be found.
It is the world that is unkind.
It is a world where no original thought you could possibly find.
In a world of pure criticism nothing is celebrated and all is unappreciated.

Then the truth is simply this.
If all is unappreciated and everyone seems to enjoy negative criticism, why do the poets bother?
Well, we bother because we must.
We must believe that in the grand scheme there will be a friend somewhere for the new.
We must believe that if we speak and dream and dare, eventually someplace, somewhere, what we speak and dream and dare will come true.
We must believe that criticism will never be so powerful as to obfuscate passion.
We must believe that even in our underappreciated and often thankless existence somehow, someway, somewhere our words still make a difference.

Nice Try

The words spoken to everyone who has ever dared and fallen
short.
The words heard by every poet whose words did not land.
The words that sting every bard whose artistry found the wrong
hands.
The words that every dreamer is petrified to hear.
The words that every adventurer does not hold dear.
The words that anyone who has ever dared and fallen short
cannot bear to hear.

Yet, there is something far worse than these words in my humble
opinion.
Yes, as far as is up to me, it would be worse to never hear these
words at all.
For, if we never hear these words it means that we never even
tried.
So, yes, I would rather try and hear nice try.
For in these words at least there is the understanding that I
dared.
For in these words at least there is the understanding that I
cared.
Yet, many turn away from this existence out of fear, but I would
rather this existence than any other that someone else might
hold dear.

For the poet knows honor more deeply than the soldier.
The poet needs no sword by which to wage his war.
The poet exists for the sake of existing.
The poet dreams because to not dream would be to stop living.
The poet may be afraid of hearing nice try, yes, but he will try,
nonetheless.
For even if their art is rejected and they are made into dust they
know honor without ever having known blood lust.

Nice try, yes nice try indeed.
The try of a poet whose words did not land.
The try of a bard whose artistry found the wrong hands.
The try of every dreamer.
The try of every adventurer.
The try of everyone who has ever dared, fallen short, and risen
again.
Yes, a nice try indeed.
Yes, a nice try at living instead of capitulating to fear and greed.

Who

A question so often asked by every poet by themselves is who
we are?
I desperately wish I could even provide the slightest semblance of
a somewhat rational response.
The truth is that much like anyone that has ever been, I doubt
that any poet can claim to know who we are meant to be.
For some of us, our art is an outlet for our pain.
For others of us, it is how we bring joy to those we care most
about.
Then again, for many more of us our writing is the one hobby we
cannot hope to live without.
Therefore, to be a poet may very well be to not ever truly know
who you are.

Then you might say, "If I do not know who I am, then how can I
be who I ought to become?"
Therein lies the truth that every poet does know; a secret that
lands on the lips sweeter than rum.
The secret of becoming and being is a simple answer, one and the
same.
To become who you ought to be, chase after your heart's flame.
For by chasing this flame you assure yourself a sworn oath of
self-honesty.
In chasing this flame, you guarantee you will become who you
ought to be.

Yes, though the answer of who anyone is has never found a good response that does not mean we should ignore the question entirely.
We should however live not trying to answer that question but rather trying to live up to it.
To desire to know who we are is to admit we care about what we accomplish.
To care about what we accomplish is to build a legacy for when our hourglass sand has run.
Yes, who we are is not a question I believe that we are meant to answer.
That question will be answered by those who knew us and lived on.
If you ask me who we poets are, then I would tell you this: we are the dreamers living each day knowing it is a sacred gift.

Fools Who Dream

Ultimately, being a poet is to see the world not as it currently is,
but as what it could be.
To look at the sky and see not just the sky, but all the stories
painted in the clouds.
To gaze into someone's eyes and see not just a pair of eyes but a
soul.
To hear someone's voice and hear not just a voice but a
symphony.
Ultimately, being a poet is to see the world not as it currently is,
but as what it could be.

Being a poet is finding beauty in what others see as plain.
From the rising of the sun to the setting of the same.
From the whisper of the wind and the trickling of the rain.
From the quiet moments of life so often taken in vain.
Being a poet is finding beauty in what others see as plain.

To be a poet is to find truth in between the clouded lies we are
told.
In the hidden expressions amongst friends hiding a story
between themselves.
In the silent moments shared between two hearts that cannot
find the words.
In the forgotten memories of time past long ago.
To be a poet is to find truth in between the clouded lies we are
told.

As poets we are bound to desire freedom.
The freedom to dream beyond what we currently see.
The freedom to hope beyond what we currently have.
The freedom to dare beyond what we currently hold.
As poets we are bound to desire freedom.

Most of all, poets are bound to chase after love.
The love of adoring readers.
The love written in between the pages of our art.
The love we carry within our hearts.
Most of all, poets are bound to chase after love.

Ultimately, being a poet is to see what others cannot.
To be a poet is to chase after beauty, truth, freedom, and love.
To be a poet is to be both in the crowd and uniquely set apart.
To be a poet is to be a fool who dreams within a foolish heart.
Ultimately, being a poet is to see what others cannot.

BOLD

For A Dream

Doubt is the greatest evil secondary only to fear.
It rips apart greatness and brings nothing except for tears.
Doubt carries in its wake only ruin.
It destroys excellence before it can begin.

Within doubt there is no goodness or light.
Within doubt there is no ability to fight.
Within doubt all hope is lost.
Within doubt everything is sold and often stolen at a ridiculous cost.

Due to this, it is necessary for us to be bold.
To be bold for our dreams.
To be bold for our beliefs.
To be bold for the sake of being bold.

We must never let doubt take away what we hold dear.
We must never allow ourselves to be reduced by fear.
We must always chase towards the stars.
We must always be bold for our dreams and everything we are.

For A Friend

The greatest strength we will ever experience often does not come from within ourselves.
This strength is born from the will of someone else.
It is the strength of someone believing in us when we cannot believe in ourselves.
It is the strength of the faith and boldness we borrow for a moment from someone else.

Therefore, I say to you: "Let us all be bold for our friends."
Let us help them reach their journey's end.
Let us lend them a hand when they are faltering.
Let them find us by their side if they should be wandering.

We know as a truth that not all who wander are lost.
We know as a truth that the greatest treasures are often found at a great cost.
This is why we must make sure our friends never pay this cost alone.
This is why we must make sure our friends can, in us, find a home.

For if our friends have lost their voice then we find ourselves
with only one choice.
We are given the choice to give a voice to the voiceless.
We are given a choice to fight a battle that is not our own but that
we cannot ignore.
We are given a choice to go to war.

Yes, we are going to war for a friend.
We are going to fight for them until the end.
We will be bold on their behalf.
We will allow them to lean on us and for them we will be a strong
staff.

The greatest strength we will ever experience does not come
from within ourselves.
This strength is borne from the will of someone else.
It is the strength of someone believing in us when we cannot
believe in ourselves.
It is the strength of the faith and boldness we borrow for a
moment from someone else.

No Fear Here

Let me for a moment impart on you the wisdom of fearless living.
Yes, the wisdom to live your life without any fear.
To understand that fear is inherently the greatest roadblock you will ever face.
To know that within fear there simply is not and never will be any faith.

Fear is not a motivator, nor does it serve any good purpose.
All fear can do is bring upon a treacherous blindness.
If you would not ask a drunkard to deliver you from an addiction to beer, why then do you ask fear to deliver you from the evil that is near?
If you choose to live in fear, then tell me what good could possibly come to bear?

All fear does is paralyze us or drive us forward for the wrong reasons.
It chokes the very voice of reason in our minds.
Fear causes us to be blind.
Fear does nothing except stir up a frenzy within our minds.

To live fearlessly is to live bold.
To live fearlessly is to accomplish dreams and many stories still yet untold.
To live fearlessly is to hold onto the pillar of faith.
To live fearlessly is to allow love and faith to take hold of your soul.

Therefore, I hope you will choose along with me to live without fear.
I pray you would choose to live constantly saying about your life "THERE IS NO FEAR HERE!"

Whom Shall I Fear

The answer to this is: no one.
Fear absolutely no one.
Never let anyone bring a veil of darkness over your eyes and your life.
Never let the foundation of your life be shaken.

See, if you know who goes before you and stands beside, then you know the battle is already won.
Though it may look like you're surrounded be assured you are surrounded by allies and not enemies.
In every battle you have fought or will ever fight the outcome has been determined long ago.
When you ask yourself, "Whom shall I fear?" respond saying, "I fear no one."

Live knowing that no principalities or powers can overtake you.
Live knowing that no weapon that was, is, or will be can overcome you.
Live knowing that even if you cannot see the end from the beginning the end has already been made to work for your good.
Live knowing that every door you will ever need to walk through has already been opened for you.

When you ask yourself, "Who do I fear?" answer that you fear no one.
Believe that what and who resides in you will always be more powerful than anything you could ever possibly face.
If even in death you have won eternity, then it stands to reason that no matter what, you can start every battle saying, "This is a battle I have already won."

One More Move

The most overused and ill-used phrase in the English language is
    checkmate.
It is used when we are supposed to be completely out of options.
Yet, the skilled at living life will always remember one fact.
The unskilled will always forget to check if the king has one
    more move.

Yes, though it may look like we are surrounded often we have one
    more move that will change the tide completely.
We have one more move that will re-open all the options we
    thought previously closed.
We have one more move that will place us right back on top.
Yes, even when we are surrounded, we should always allow
    ourselves to believe we have one more move.

Those who would tell us checkmate often jump their starting
    gun out of an abundance of desire to see us fail.
It is in the moment when we hear checkmate that we must step
    back and remember, "If my King still stands, then the game is
    not yet over."
For at this junction of our lives we must recall that while we can
    think, while we can walk, while we can stand, and while we
    can talk, our dreams are still able to come true.
There may be such a thing as checkmate on a chess board, but
    in life we will always have one more move if we are willing to
    find it.

Yes, we will always find ourselves with one more move.

We will have one more move that we had previously ignored.

We will have one more move which for a rainy day we have
stored.

Yes, even in the moment where we should be stuck in checkmate,
we can boldly look at the boards of our lives and say, "I have
ONE MORE MOVE!"

IN LOVE

Firestorm (Dove 2)

Few wonders can shine brighter than lightning.
Fewer can make it stop in its tracks; fewer make it lie on its back.
It's funny then, how you did that to me.
Funny, how you chilled me straight through my bones and
through my heart and through my core.
Yet, it wasn't exactly a chill.
No, it was a burning, a piercing, a raging, tempestuous fire.
A firestorm to match my lightning strike.
A bright, all-encompassing, and piercing sight that I couldn't
ignore.

Yes, you only you.
My still warmth.
Yes, you only you.
My bright light.
Yes, you only you.
My firestorm.

Please don't leave me; keep shining through the night.
I'm not sure I can get through my story if you decide to leave
tonight.
I'm not sure that I want to say goodbye.
Please just let me dream here for a while.
Let me believe that this might last.
I know I don't know the right words to say.
Even if I did it wouldn't change anything.
Storms like you just don't last.
So, you burnt out; I say goodbye.
There's just a quiet and lonely embrace for a lone lightning strike
in the dark night sky.

One Dance

We shared a dance.
We floated on angels' breath.
Our hearts were one.
Our minds worked in tandem.

Then the music took us away.
We were lost but we were found all at once.
In the future and in the past all that could be or was.

Then that song started to fade away.
All that remained was you and I and memory.
Then we stepped away.
We stepped away from that dance floor.

Suddenly the time was running away.
Yet, it didn't matter because we were both artists and time means
nothing to us anyway.
It doesn't slip through our fingers; we can freeze it any day.
It's our nature to make time obey.
To make it freeze so we can remember the one dance we shared
that day.

Looking Over

Please tell me why all these shining lights could never shine as
bright as your eyes.
Also, could you tell me why I'm trapped in their skies?
Love, don't you know you're everything that I want?
Oh, can't you give me all the love from your heart.
My firestorm, my secret eternal love.
Ah, it's plain to see you're the one that I love.

So, as you look over and I look back we are both lost.
Yes, lost in the melody of the song in our hearts.
Maybe it's all right; we can stay here for a while.
Please tell me if we can stay lost here for a while.
Hold me and tell me that we're going to be fine.
Only then might I be brave enough to go into the night.
Yes, this all ran through my mind as you looked over, but I didn't
go over to you that night.

One Night

Part of me knows I should have kept you in my memories.
I guess I really went and ruined everything.
She was looking over her eyes, calling to my heart.
Ready as I was to go to her, I couldn't leave you.
Call it luck, call it lust, call it love but I was stuck.
Held back by the twisted fate of our broken love.
Even still, I wish I had left you there before all the misery.
Still, I hardly doubt that would have changed anything.
Then again who knows?
Really, I guess we were just passing time.
All of this while I sat with you, but I couldn't escape her eyes that
one summer night.

An Artist's Goodbye

We both have dreams that we need to chase.
We both have fears that we need to face.
There are places that we must be.
There are bright lights that we must see.

So, I guess this is goodbye.
We let each other go so we can fly.
There's no other way for us.
We've burned up all our trust.
There's nothing left to say.
So, I'm writing this to say goodbye.

I want you to go and see the world.
I want you to go and change it too.
You deserve so much more than all there is.
You deserve to have a life of bliss.

So, I know this is goodbye.
I also know how hard you tried.
Still, artists are meant to fly.
So, please go fly high above the sky.
It's time that we say goodbye.

Holding On

There are memories that never fade.
There are moments that do not respect time.
The most beautiful memories are made when no plan is laid.

Time comes back each time our song is played.
Each measure of it sounds like a perfect rhyme.
There are memories that never fade.

I remember standing by your side unafraid.
I remember walking along with your hand in mine.
The most beautiful memories are made when no plan is laid.

The time we danced together and along we swayed.
Swaying to the careful rhythm of a delicate chime.
There are memories that never fade.

There are memories that cut deeper than any blade.
There are moments unspeakable and frozen in time.
The most beautiful memories are made when no plan is laid.
From gifts given from afar on Christmas day.
From words spoken from this heart of mine.
There are memories that never fade.
The most beautiful memories are made when no plan is laid.

Letting Go

Sometimes, we must let our memories fade.
Sometimes, it's best to let go.
We must free the memories we make.

Certain memories are not meant to be replayed.
Certain treasures are best let go.
Sometimes we must let our memories fade.

There comes a time when our memory must be betrayed.
A time where we bury our feelings deep below.
We must free the memories we make.

We bury them deep below because we're afraid.
Afraid of what these memories show.
Sometimes we must let our memories fade.

So, we bury our memories, and, in a grave, they're laid.
We bury against what we should let go.
We must free the memories we make.

Not all love is meant to last forever until we've aged.
Yet, there's still beauty in love even when it's let go.
Sometimes we must let our memories fade.
We must free the memories we make.

New Beginnings

Poets love to say we have love all figured out.
It is the one theme we say is easy to write about.
Yes, love poetry is fun to write and to read.
Yet, poets struggle to let love lead.

It is true that poets know all about love.
We know all about love, but we shy away from it.
It is easier when love is just a theme.
It is terrifying when love becomes our dream.

Poets have love all figured out until we find ourselves in it.
In that moment suddenly, we know nothing.
Our once silver tongue has turned to lead.
We scramble for any coherent thought in our heads.

He had love all figured out, or so he thought.
Then he heard a voice of silk paired to a laugh as warm as
the sun.
Then he saw the rays of that sun streaming through the waves in
her hair.
He was entranced by the gold of her honey brown eyes.

Yes, the poet had love all figured out until he was in it.
At that moment he said, "What more is there to write when
poetry comes to life?"
The poet had to let life lead him on.
He told life, "Give me a new beginning if it means she will be here
from now on."

JOYFUL

Storm Cloud

Life is beautiful in every sense.
From the rise of the sun to the fall of the same.
The warm summer breeze and frigid winter rain.
Life is beautiful in every way.

Life is beautiful in every sense.
From the days that go by, and the memories forever etched in our halls of fame.
The people we meet along the way are far too many to name.
Life is beautiful in every way.

Life is beautiful in every sense.
From the winter storms spent inside playing a game.
The hours spent that burned rapidly like a flame.
Life is beautiful in every way.

Life is beautiful in every sense.
From friends like you who bring a smile to my face.
The laughter and joy that runs at a marvelous pace.
So please remember always, but especially today.
Life is beautiful in every way.

Little Mouse

There exists a unique hidden strength that some own.
A quiet, wild torrential show of force.
Yet this force stays in the shadows.
It is unknown except for the few who know it exists.

This hidden strength has been named boldness.
A strong, unwavering, almost risky confidence.
Yet, this strength often goes unnoticed.
It is only us few that are blessed to know it.

This thing we call boldness is proved to all best by artists.
An artist putting up their work for the world to judge.
Yes, a little mouse face to face with the elephant of criticism.
Still, these artists say, "Love me or hate me, I'm here to stay."

Then I tell you all; here is what I say.
I'm joyful for the little mice that present themselves before the world boldly.
Yes, joyful, not just grateful that there are strong yet quiet souls willing to risk everything.
It makes me happy to know that this world hasn't yet beat everyone down.

On The Pier

Quiet conversations held with only the eyes.
The conversations' words hold no lies.
Two hearts beating together as one.
Two people walking along watching the setting sun.

In the silence they say a million words.
Their emotions hit each other like clashing swords.
Walking along the pier they watch as the stars shimmer across
the sea.
They begin to dream of what they can be.

The quiet conversations continue and neither he nor she wants
them to end.
So, they continue losing themselves in their eyes.
They smile at each other under the lavish Pacific sky.
They are joyful to share a moment in what they know will
someday be time gone by.

Looking Out

The ocean holds the memories of all she has ever held.
Perhaps that is why you ran from her embrace.
You did not want your memories held by anything except your heart.
For if only you held them, they would be the start.
The start of whatever story you wish to tell.

The one you first wrote that day in the sand.
The one you thought no one was paying attention to.

The ocean gleamed as the sun streamed through the waves in your hair.
A breeze flowed through the space between two artists.
One uses the ocean to lose his memory and forget.
The other stayed away from the ocean so she could remember.
In one space a story dying and being born.

The story of two hearts deaf to the call they made to each other.
The story of hearts beating for one another.
The story of the purest object in the world.
The story of moments shared quietly as two people look over at each other and then out across the ocean and smile.

An Evening in Roma

I think of you as I watch the sunset over the sea.
A calm serenity envelops me in this ancient villa.
Then I fade into the ancient tapestry of Roma.
Yes, a tapestry of legends and heroes and myths.
A quilt telling what was and leaving space for what still may be.
In this old city I remember us and all our stories.
I remember our beginning our middle and our end.
The smiles we once shared are now memories.
The memories of a heart that one day you helped love again.
The hopes and dreams and all you inspired live on.
Even if you are far from where I now belong.
I remember you now more that you are gone.
I still sing what was once our song.
That song held the key to both our hearts.
Two hearts forever connected by an evening in Roma.
Two hearts forever connected by an evening in Roma.
That song held the key to both our hearts.
I still sing what was once our song.
I remember you now more that you are gone.
Even if you are far from where I now belong.
The hopes and dreams and all you inspired live on.
The memories of a heart that one day you helped love again.
The smiles we once shared are now memories.
I remember our beginning our middle and our end.
In this old city I remember us and all our stories.
A quilt telling what was and leaving space for what still may be.
Yes, a tapestry of legends and heroes and myths.
Then I fade into the ancient tapestry of Roma.
A calm serenity envelops me in this ancient villa.
I think of you as I watch the sunset over the sea.

AT PEACE

With Others

Forgiveness is the most powerful force we know.
To forgive each other is to set ourselves free.
Our ability to forgive is the measure of who we are.
Some of us forgive freely.
Some of us struggle to forgive at all.
Yet, forgiveness gives us the soundest peace we will ever know.
Forgiveness gives our souls the deepest rest.
When we forgive, we unleash something incredibly powerful.
We unleash our belief in the good of others.
A belief that the good they have can rebuild the world.
To rebuild the world in the image of love.
To live at peace with others.
To walk hand in hand as brothers.
To walk hand in hand as brothers.
To live at peace with others.
To rebuild the world in the image of love.
A belief that the good they have can rebuild the world.
We unleash our belief in the good of others.
When we forgive, we unleash something incredibly powerful.
Forgiveness gives our souls the deepest rest.
Yet, forgiveness gives us the soundest peace we will ever know.
Some of us struggle to forgive at all.
Some of us forgive freely.
How much we forgive is the quiet definition of who we are.
It is the expression of the best parts of us.
Our ability to forgive is the measure of who we are.
To forgive each other is to set ourselves free.
Forgiveness is the most powerful force we know.

With Yourself

To live is to know who you are.
It is being at peace with your potential.
Not only being at peace with it but loving it.
Most of all make sure to love your heart.
Protect and guard its entrance.
Be careful what you allow to enter.
Do not make your heart impenetrable.
Make sure you let the right people in.
Let in those who bring you peace.
Still, the most important person to be at peace with is yourself.
Forgive yourself for your shortcomings and relish your successes.
Only when you are at peace with yourself can you achieve greatly.
You are the only one with an obligation to believe in yourself.
Therefore, I tell you to henceforth, believe.
Believe in yourself and be at peace.
Believe in yourself and be at peace.
Therefore, I tell you to henceforth, believe.
You are the only one with an obligation to believe in yourself.
Only when you are at peace with yourself can you achieve greatly.
Forgive yourself for your shortcomings and relish your successes.
Still, the most important person to be at peace with is yourself.
Let in those who bring you peace.
Make sure you let the right people in.
Do not make your heart impenetrable.
Be careful what you allow to enter.
Protect and guard its entrance.
Most of all make sure to love your heart.
Not only being at peace with it but loving it.
It is being at peace with your potential.
To live is to know who you are.

In Life

Do not simply live, thrive.
Live each day to the fullest.
Savor each breath.
Listen more than you speak and speak as much as you can.
Appreciate beauty every moment you have.
Love passionately and in earnest.
Care deeply and in truth.
Appreciate every moment for what it is.
Pay no mind to what it is not.
Be mindful not to miss forests for trees.
Say what you mean and mean what you say.
When you meet someone extraordinary, do not let them go.
If you must let them, go, do it with joy.
Be happy you met someone and loved them enough to do so.
Being happy life gave you peace enough to love boldly.
Being happy life gave you peace enough to love boldly.
Be happy you met someone and loved them enough to do so.
If you must let them, go, do it with joy.
When you meet someone extraordinary, do not let them go.
Say what you mean and mean what you say.
Be mindful not to miss forests for trees.
Pay no mind to what is not.
Appreciate every moment for what it is.
Care deeply and in truth.
Love passionately and in earnest.
Appreciate beauty every moment you have.
Listen more than you speak and speak as much as you can.
Savor each breath.
Live each day to the fullest.
Do not simply live, thrive.

In The Present

Today is a gift.
Yesterday has been carried away.
Tomorrow is still being written.
Truly, there is no time like the present.
Only the present is in our control.
If we learned from yesterday, then we can shape today.
In shaping today, we can build tomorrow.
Yet, to shape tomorrow, we must live today.
We must appreciate the gift in our hands.
The gift of life we experience with each breath.
The soft breeze whispering our lives back to us.
Let us not forget the sun lighting our paths.
Let us not forget the people we meet on those paths.
Let us remember to smile for life's charms.
Let us remember to be at peace in the present.
Let us remember to be at peace in the present.
Let us remember to smile for life's charms.
Let us not forget the people we meet on those paths.
Let us not forget the sun lighting our paths.
The soft breeze whispering our lives back to us.
The gift of life we experience with each breath.
We must appreciate the gift in our hands.
Yet, to shape tomorrow, we must live today.
In shaping today, we can build tomorrow.
If we learned from yesterday, then we can shape today.
Only the present is in our control.
Truly, there is no time like the present.
Tomorrow is still being written.
Yesterday has been carried away.
Today is a gift.

In Tomorrow

The future is yours to write.
Your story belongs to you.
Make it a good one.
Fill it with adventure.
Live this life without fear.
Enjoy every moment.
Treasure very breath.
Experience every sunrise.
Adore every sky.
As much as it is up to you, be at peace.
Be at peace with yourself, with others, in life, today and tomorrow.
Life is beautiful and worth living.
Life is a precious gift.
Within life, there are many more gifts.
Yes, the sun will always come out tomorrow.
Yes, the sun will always come out tomorrow.
Within life, there are many more gifts.
Life is a precious gift.
Life is beautiful and worth living.
Be at peace with yourself, with others, in life, today and tomorrow.
As much as it is up to you, be at peace.
Adore every sky.
Experience every sunrise.
Treasure every breath.
Enjoy every moment.
Live this life without fear.
Fill it with adventure.
Make it a good one.
Your story belongs to you.
The future is yours to write.

FAITHFUL

In a Moment

Hold on tight and do not let go.
The moment you prayed for has arrived.
Just for a moment, let your heart show.

You are capable of far more than you know.
You have fought and lived.
Hold on tight and do not let go.

Keep dreaming, ready the ground, and sow.
Now, take heart so you can say you thrived.
Just for a moment, let your heart show.

Live boldly and do not lay low.
The moment for laying low is gone; the moment for living has
arrived.
Hold on tight and do not let go.

Dream and dream boldly wherever you go.
Make sure the best is for what you strived.
Just for a moment, let your heart show.

Take care of this moment, and do not let it go.
Have faith that when it is over you will have won and lived.
Hold on tight and do not let go.
Just for a moment, let your heart show.

Beyond Reason

Sometimes, faith goes beyond reason.
It believes in what is impossible to see.
Still, faith must be kept no matter the season.

It must be kept in and out of season.
It must be kept however tired we may be.
Sometimes, faith goes beyond reason.

It goes with us who keep believing.
It stays even when we are trapped and not free.
Still, faith must be kept no matter the season.

Kept, because even if we are trapped it can release us from prison.
Faith, above anything else, is the key.
Sometimes, faith goes beyond reason.

I admit it is a habit that is difficult to find ease in.
It is hard to believe in what we cannot see.
Still, faith must be kept no matter the season.

It will be our guide in staying or leaving.
It will be the only thing to truly set us free.
Sometimes, faith goes beyond reason.
Still, faith must be kept no matter the season.

Without Evidence

If faith must be blind, then let it be blind.
Let it exist in the deepest parts of our beings.
At times, blind faith does more than an open mind.

A blind faith often helps us leave the past behind.
It gives us hope for the results we are not seeing.
If faith must be blind, then let it be blind.

Let it exist despite the doubts in our minds.
When the storms of life come let it be the rock on which we are
leaning.
At times, blind faith does more than an open mind.

It sets us free and allows us to be kind.
It keeps our hearts in line with hope that is freeing.
If faith must be blind, then let it be blind.

If nothing else, let it be the treasure that we find.
Let it be what we hold onto when life cuts us, and we are
bleeding.
At times, blind faith does more than an open mind.

It does good because in it there is no fear you can find.
It does good because it makes hearts blazing.
If faith must be blind, then let it be blind.
At times, blind faith does more than an open mind.

Against All Odds

Your dream is your dream, regardless of who doubts.
Your dream will keep you going day in and day out.
Hold onto it even through life's droughts.

Keep it always at the forefront of your thoughts.
Though the troubles of life may scream and shout.
Your dream is your dream, regardless of who doubts.

It will be with you every step, every turn, for all the roundabouts.
Keep it near your heart and never doubt.
Hold onto it even through life's droughts.

Through all the ups, downs, ins, and outs.
Through every moment you live from here on out.
Your dream is your dream, regardless of who doubts.

Against every loss, even if a few of them are routs.
Against every dark shadow life may cast here, there, and about.
Hold onto it even through life's droughts.

Never let it go no matter who shouts.
Let it be what you simply will not live without.
Your dream is your dream regardless of who doubts.
Hold onto it even through life's droughts.

For a Friend

Believe in and for your friends.
Trust in their hearts.
Good ones will stick around to the very end.

They will be there until for them time sends.
They will be there at the start.
Believe in and for your friends.

Treasure them and if any trouble arises make amends.
Treasure them; they are works of art.
Good ones will stick around to the very end.

They will always have a hand to lend.
Love from them will never depart.
Believe in and for your friends.

Let theirs be the hearts you defend.
Defend their hearts against every fiery dart.
Good ones will stick around to the very end.

It is a gift to be surrounded by good friends.
It is a gift to be loved purely of heart.
Believe in and for your friends.
Good ones will stick around to the very end.

For Love

Love is beauty, love is kind.
It is treasure.
Love is the finest treasure you will ever find.

Love is patiently designed.
It does not apply pressure.
Love is beauty, love is kind.

Love never leaves us in a bind.
It is something we cannot measure.
Love is the finest treasure you will ever find.

Love is decided and refined.
It stays strong through whatever.
Love is beauty, love is kind.

Love can never be undermined.
You will never find something better.
Love is the finest treasure you will ever find.

Love is everything good about life intertwined.
Love goes on forever.
Love is beauty, love is kind.
Love is the finest treasure you will ever find.

Forever

Never, ever, lose faith; keep it forever.
Believe in what it can do.
Nurture it, defend it, protect it: FOREVER.

Hold it firmly and never let it go, never!
Hold onto it for me and for you.
Never, ever lose faith; keep it FOREVER.

It can guide you through whatever.
Believe that what you have faith in will come true.
Nurture it, defend it, protect it: FOREVER.

Faith has a way of being so very clever.
If nothing else let faith be what you pursue.
Never, ever lose faith; keep it FOREVER.

Faith is a tie you should never sever.
Believe that faith can always start something new.
Nurture it, defend it, protect it: FOREVER.

Have faith in every endeavor.
Hold onto faith no matter what you do.
Never, ever lose faith; keep it FOREVER.
Nurture it, defend it, protect it, FOREVER.

HOPEFUL

Moonlight Talking

I find myself lost between the moon and New York City.
I am thinking about you.
I am remembering everything we have been through.
All the memories are as beautiful as you.
So, I will stay talking to the moon.
I'll tell her every single story I have about you.
I'll tell her about the memories and a few dreams too.
I'll tell her every wonderful dream I've ever had about you.
Yes, it's crazy but that's what I'll do.
I'll fall in love and find my way back to New York City.
I'll find my way back to the moon.
Yes, I'm sure that's where I'll find you.
Oh, all the finest dreams end up at the moon and New York City.
So, I'm sure that when I get there you'll be there too.

City of Stars

There is something calming about this city in the dead of night.
A city filled with artists of every style.
One with the stars in the sky and on the ground.
There is a sense of wonder and beauty all around.
A song plays and its sound transports you away.
One almost wonders how not to fall in love here.
There are hopes and dreams in every breath.
A breath of excitement carried by the wind over the sea.
One moment of time held in place like walking through a memory.
One moment of time held in place like walking through a memory.
A breath of excitement carried by the wind over the sea.
There are hopes and dreams in every breath.
One almost wonders how not to fall in love here.
A song plays and its sound transports you away.
There is a sense of wonder and beauty all around.
One with stars in the sky and on the ground.
A city filled with artists of every style.
There is something calming about this city in the dead of night.

Beyond The Sea

There is a place that waits for me.
A small little island across the sea.
The memories of her and I.
They wait for me there in that Caribbean sky.

Sunrises await her and I.
Sunsets will come as we pass by.
Yet, all of this existed in the past.
Our story ended long ago, and in stone, it is cast.

So, there is a place that no longer waits for me.
There is no little island across the sea.
The memories of her and I are memories no more.
No, as with everything they became the present story of living I
hope to live forevermore.

Over The Ocean

Some of the best shared memories form when two hearts are thousands of miles apart.
They are formed by threads of emotions carried by the ocean breeze.
They are given life by the wind rustling between the trees.
Two hearts find themselves completely bare.
They are both hopeful, scared, and unprepared.
They are making promises to each other as their lives are shared.
Though right now they are an ocean apart.
They are two hearts talking about becoming one.
They are two dreamers flying towards the sun.
They are two vagabonds who in each other have found a home.
They are two bohemians who since finding each other now have hope in not facing this life alone.

One Day

One day, we shall live in the world we built.
The world we always dreamed of.
The world where love knows no bounds.
The world filled with poets and artists and plays.
Oh, what a wonder that will be.
Oh, yes, what a delight when wonder will be free.

One day we shall live in the world we built.
A world built because we held on dearly to hope.
A world built on the promises we kept.
A world built on the love and memories we shared.
Yes, a place where a bright dawn follows a calm night.
Yes, a place where all the dreams we dream take flight.

One day we shall live in the world we built.
Some world where sorrow no longer takes any hold.
Some world where heartbreak is no more.
Some world where pain and loss are in the past.
Ah, that will be a wonderful symphony of sound.
Ah, the sounds of laughter and comradery all around.

One day, we shall live in the world we built.
The world where delight and wonder are free.
A world where night falls, dawn breaks, and dreams fly.
Some world where joy and laughter are the only sounds.
One day, we shall live in the world we built.

Sometimes (Dove 3)

Come with me if you can and remember all we have been
through.
Hold me in your arms again, so the memories can return.
Allow me to get lost just one last time in your eyes.
Set my soul on fire.

You are capable of more than I could ever fathom.
One day I hope you will believe in yourself as much as I believe
in you.
Until that day I hope you will at least believe that I believe in you.
Really, I now and forever will believe in you and all you can do.

Darling, in case I have not told you, you are the inspiration.
Racing through my mind.
Every word reflects you.
All I've ever written a part of you from my heart.
Memories that became my art.

There's More

I find myself dreaming again.
Yet, more than dreaming, I am reminiscing.
I recall moments of freedom, beauty, truth, and love.
Moments of wonder so unexplainable I could hardly speak.
Most of all, I remember moments in time when time stood still.
In those moments, the future seemed endless.
In those moments it was as if I held the world in my hands.
Nowadays it is those moments that lead me to believe there is
more to this life.
Time waits for no man, but the future is mine for the taking.
Every moment, every thought, every dream will come true if I
let it.
So, I look ahead to my future whilst remembering the beauty of
my past.
My heart charges full steam ahead.
Today and always my dreams fill my head.
Even though the past shone brightly, the future shines like
the sun.
There are more dreams I must dream.
There is more love I must give.
There is more life I must live.

Dream Forward

If there is more life for me to live, then the same is true for you.
You also have more love to give.
It is also true that you have barely started to dream.
Your future will shine brightly like the sun as your glistening past remembers all you have done.
Keep letting wild dreams fill your head.
Keep letting your heart charge full steam ahead.
Keep looking towards tomorrow while you yearn for the beauty of yesterday.
I believe that all your dreams will come true.
Time does not wait, but the future waits for you.
Now and forever believe in the beauty of life.
Believe that the world is yours for the taking.
Believe that the world can and should be endlessly beautiful.
Most of all, allow yourself to slow down now and then.
Slow down and appreciate every breathtaking sight and moment.
Slow down and appreciate freedom, beauty, truth, and love.
Dream forward as you love what is making sure to look forward to what can be.
Dream forward and live beautifully.

Instagram: @LightningPublications
Twitter: @LightningPub18
Email: cordero1804@gmail.com